Zen Master Poems

The New Wisdom Poems series was conceived as a way of offering contemporary Buddhist poetry that has been vetted for the quality of its craft and the integrity of its wisdom. The series aims to cultivate and give a platform to the living Buddhist poets who carry Buddhist literary traditions forward and whose voices reflect the lives and practices of modern readers.

The editors wish to thank Florence Caplow, Tsering Wangmo Dhompa, Patrick Donnelly, Margaret Gibson, Jane Hirshfeld, Terrance Keenan, Peter Levitt, Dave O'Neal, and Peter Schireson, who offered valuable feedback on submissions and on the larger series identity. Without this outstanding group of readers, this first volume of the *New Wisdom Poems* series would never have taken flight.

zen master poems

Dick Allen

Wisdom

Wisdom Publications
199 Elm Street
Somerville, MA 02144 USA
wisdompubs.org

Library of Congress Cataloging-in-Publication Data
Names: Allen, Dick, 1939– author.
Title: Zen Master Poems / by Dick Allen.
Description: Somerville, MA : Wisdom Publications, [2016] | Series:
    New Wisdom Poems
Identifiers: LCCN 2015041218 (print) | LCCN 2015041727 (ebook) | ISBN
    9781614292999 (pbk. : acid-free paper) | ISBN 161429299X (pbk. : acid-
    free paper) | ISBN 9781614293200 (ebook) | ISBN 1614293201 (ebook)
Subjects: LCSH: Zen poetry, American. | Koans.
Classification: LCC PS3551.L3922 A6 2016 (print) | LCC PS3551.L3922 (ebook) |
    DC 811/.54—dc23
LC record available at http://lccn.loc.gov/2015041218

ISBN 978-1-61429-299-9   ebook ISBN 978-1-61429-320-0
20 19 18 17 16   5 4 3 2 1

Cover and interior design by Gopa&Ted2, Inc.
Set in Bembo Std 11 pt./13.7. pt.

to Lori
throughout this passage here

Table of Contents

Preface

I.

Composing these poems over these past twenty years or so, unexpectedly and sometimes inexplicably I discovered myself writing in the voice of one who's a Zen Master, one as devoted as I am to traditional Buddhist scripture and to taking a meaningful and somewhat offbeat way through life.

For a long time I'd studied koans in the *Blue Cliff Record*. I'd repeatedly walked through the Asian section of the Yale Art Museum. I'd shunned chocolate malted milkshakes, then indulged in them. Through these practices and others, I became more and more able to hear the Zen Master. At times in a semi-trance, at times in a willed act of identification, I found these poems. More accurately, they found me.

The Zen Master is my alterego, my doppelganger, a persona.

II.

Working with a persona has to do with empathy—with thinking and feeling as another might think and feel. It calls upon what John Keats famously called "negative capability": "when a man is capable of being in uncertainties, mysteries, doubts, without any irritable reaching after fact and reason."

Empathy and negative capability seem to me yoked to compassion and mindfulness.

And, in Zen, compassion and mindfulness may lead to realizations about how caring and right intention unveil that which wasn't hidden at all, perhaps a look of puzzlement in shadows behind a confident face.

You can see what compelled me.

Many of the Zen Master poems are drawn from such realizations as well as from the Zen Master's journey and struggle (and my journey and struggle and maybe yours) to push through cobwebs and mist, to walk down puzzling metropolitan streets… and to experience if not enlightenment then at least a few glimmers of it.

As the poems arrive from numerous compass points and at least one hillside, they repeatedly imply that I should slow down, be mindful, accept the Present, not take myself too seriously. Sometimes I'm able to listen. At other times I foolishly hum or forget to skip stones across Thrushwood Lake.

How might one live a life awakened by the teachings of Zen? More specifically, how does one live calmly and with perspective in an America of media blitz and cell phone insistence? How does one lean back in a computer chair and hear temple bells ring in South Dakota?

III.

A Zen Master poem may act as a koan to be realized or an *enso* to be completed.

A Zen Master, having eaten a blueberry muffin and drunk a cup of tea, might say of a poem, "Ponder it. Puzzle it. Let it live within you."

IV.

My personal roots in Buddhism go back to my childhood upbringing in the 1940s village of Round Lake, New York. There my town postmaster father had befriended Mr. Hirohara. Behind his small house, Mr. Hirohara had created a small Japanese garden. What I know now to be a Zen Buddhist-influenced garden was the most beautiful thing I'd ever seen.

In high school I discovered and read the works of Henry David Thoreau and Ralph Waldo Emerson. The Transcendentalism of these Massachusetts writers took me to their own readings in Buddhist literature.

As an undergraduate at Syracuse University, I heard and met and spoke briefly with Alan Watts. Earlier I'd read his *The Way of Zen* and many, many essays by D. T. Suzuki.

Alan Watts's eyes are still the most intense I've ever encountered.

In the summer after my freshman year, fallen under the spell of Jack Kerouac's *On the Road* and Allen Ginsberg's *Howl*, I hitchhiked and bus- and train-rode my way around America, in search of the Beat Generation experience. I found the Co-Existence Bagel Shop and Lawrence Ferlinghetti's City Lights Bookstore, but the Beats had abandoned San Francisco that summer for Colorado, leaving only a few proto-hippies sitting around on sidewalks.

In my junior college year, I took the nation's first college credit course in Zen Buddhism, offered by Dr. Daniel Smith. We met in his apartment's living room, where we tried to sit in yoga poses and positions.

Since then I've meditated and studied Zen extensively. The Zen Master who speaks the poems in this book develops from these meditations and studies.

V.

May a Zen Master poem here or there cause you to pause or smile or sit beside an evening lake or walk a small meandering ways down a quiet road.

Dick Allen
Thrushwood Lake

The Zen Master

Heal-all, buttercups, violets—it's Spring
at Thrushwood Lake.
He must be out walking.
He walks around the lake to his left.
Then he walks around the lake to his right.
"Walking Meditation," he calls it,
"I try to notice everything.
Sometimes, I manage one petal."

To Be with a Koan

To *be* with a koan
has nothing to do with *Hamlet,*
those old jokes about small pigs
or tiny villages,
bees and beekeepers. No,
to *be* with a koan,
you must get inside it
without forcing your entry.
It's like you're lemonade powder
dissolving in water.
Something other than you
does the stirring,
but there's nothing other than you,
and after a while, nothing stirs.

When You're in Trouble

When you're in trouble,
ask, "What is this?"

You must ask it three times,
in three different ways:

What is this?
    What *is* this?
        What is *this*?

It's a question-koan, of course.

There are as many answers
as people on earth.

For instance:

1) *aizu*—the Japanese word for sign, signal.
2) an illusion with a heartbeat.
3) salt and the sea on the tongue.

It Was an Era

It was an era
                    of mystical songs.
But one stood out: the Beatles
"Let it Be"—
an almost perfect combination
of Christianity and Zen.

Let it be, let it be, let it be, let it be
is a mantra.

There will be an answer, let it be,

especially the way the song
dwindles down to nothing at the end,
but you still seem to hear the words.

How Good It Would Be

How good it would be
to not question.
Does the cat question its fur?
Does the window question sunlight pouring
    through it?
Does a blanket question how it lies upon
    the bed?

Learn how to not question
and you may yet still the mind.

Special Transmission

I heard
a special transmission.

It was as if I were a child
searching with a crystal radio,
scraping a cat's whisker across the crystal.

I read about it nowhere,
but it was pointed at me,

turning me inside out,
so that someday,
five hundred lives from now
I might become a buddha.

More likely, however,
is that I'll be a sled runner
on somebody's Flexible Flyer,
speeding down hills
under the streetlights,
snow falling lightly, like static.

A Two-Hundred-Year-Old Drinking Cup

The chair, the air, the paper, and the street,
you must be kind to them.

The chair has been much sat in.
The air has been much breathed.
This paper was once a tree
        overlooking a valley.
This street was once woodland
        mottled by sunlight.

And that cup from which you now drink,
how many times has it been lifted up,
how many times has it been tilted,
how many times has it been set down?

Its handle has felt ten thousand fingertips,
its lip has felt a thousand lips against it.

Were they softer than yours?
Were they harder?

How many past lives have you lived?

Here comes the sun.

The most expected thing you can expect
is what's unexpected.

Evocations

I like the phrases,

"at the base of the cliff,"
"deep in the forest,"
"at the edge of the field,"
"on the shore of the lake."

And

"adrift on the river,"
"obscured by the mist,"
"lost in the clouds,"
"beside the waterfall."

But also,

"lighting a candle,"
"in evening shadow
 a lone monk tolling a bell."

A Night Gas Station

A night gas station on a river road,
what could be more American?

The old lit neon sign you can almost read
    from
     a mile away
and the attendant, leaning back in one chair,
feet up on another chair,
listening like some owl.

When I Was Young

When I was young
and it was snowing as if you could hear
   wolves howling,
I used to walk deep into the forest,
under great white pines,
following deer and rabbit tracks until they
   disappeared,
or until I found, under the thickest branches,
what was almost a small dry cave or cavern
with a floor of brown needles.

There, I'd sit down,
clasping my hands around my knees
to watch snow falling.

I taught myself, for hours,
to watch snow falling.

The Strange Magic of Your Life

The strange magic of your life,
memories of the strange tree
on the strange hillside,
the tinglings of *kensho* or R. D. Laing's
theory that we all go crazy
two or three times each day:
a moment of turning your head,
a moment of feeling on your thumb the
    imprint of a coin,
or a violet petal, or clicker of a ballpoint
    pen . . .

Some enchanted evening, you may see a stranger.

. . . the strange magic everywhere around
    you
and about you
and within you—
how certain, how strange it is.

On the Raft

perfectly adrift.

On the Raft II

The trouble with you
is you carry the raft everywhere
but you've never floated upon it

and if you ever do,
once you reach the other shore,
can you leave it behind,

bobbing in the waters?

After a Heavy, Clinging Snow

After a heavy, clinging snow,
snow falling from pine trees,
I like to watch
a large rib of snow
falling from a high branch,
then how it breaks up, it cascades
through lower branches,
sometimes to fall *sudden*,
sometimes

                             slowly,

like the two types of Zen:
the flash card koan,
the settling down of zazen.

Frisbee

It's like tossing Frisbees.
You grip them
between your thumb and forefinger,
supporting the Frisbee
with three of your other fingers, then
you cock the wrist and sweep it out. The
   Frisbee
spins and *sails*. It's beautiful. The principle
is arcuate vances and turbulators.
And when it slows down,
if you've sailed it a long, long way,
it *floats*
into another's outstretched hands,
transmitted
over a crowd of disciples
and perhaps someone leaps up to catch it.

Following Another's Example

I see him around the village,
planting his karmic seeds
in every lawn—
a minor Johnny Chapman
walking Connecticut.

Carefully, he sows,
always allowing for drainage,
hoping he's fooled the slugs.

May root systems take hold!

May there be germination!

They're so fragile, he says,
especially at the start,
before the first four true leaves.

Loving wishes, quiet favors,
compassionate acts, small good deeds.

How pleasant his stooped back,
to know he's at work
over carrots and peas.

Near at hand, may great pumpkins
swell from the ground.

Dread

Dread
is like lead.
Always weighing
upon you.

Can I crawl out from under it?

Hardly likely
unless you can learn
to take things slowly,
calmly,
lightly,

in place of,
instead.

Sadness

"Vaguely dissatisfied,"
 is a good way to put it,
 another is "restless,"
 or "slightly out of sorts,"
 or "trying to put two and two together,"
"somewhat confused,"
"not quite with it,"
"never exactly here."

That feeling there was something else
you had to do,
you'd vowed to do
between your last life and this,

like live a peaceful life in the mountains,
fish in far rivers.

Lost Souls

Somewhere, they're convinced, there's
   one answer,
one horse,
one lottery number,
of which they're not yet aware

and so they wander
from one enthusiasm to the next,
one secret, one whisper,
one poetry reading in the middle of the
   night,
to another, then another—the answer
always around the next corner,
behind the next door.

Since lost souls always draw near,
they're sure
the answer will appear,
all will be made clear

possibly tomorrow,
and if not then, the day after

but just as when birds fly
they encounter the air,
so also

wherever we go and wherever we are
the answer is *here,*
already *here.*

Juice dribbling from the pear,

or maybe it's laughter.

Excuse Me

"Excuse me," the roshi said,
 removing his earphone,
"I was just listening to some *honkyoku*
 and thinking about a wandering monk
   I knew
whose passion was collecting sounds
on a Sony digital tape recorder. He played
   me
raindrops,
wind high in the Rockies, surging through
   aspens,
the magnified sound
of an ant climbing a rock wall.
Such sounds!
Boring, enlightening.
But my favorite sound
was of his voice, explaining
the sound of hand-drawn curtains
on an old curtain rod,
metal scraping metal, very lightly."

Of the Ten Thousand Things

Of the ten thousand things
you don't have to know,
here are seven:

How to not fall over when leaning against the wind.
How to dissolve a slug with sea salt.
How to catch a tiger by its toe.
How to flip a flapjack.
How to find your way to San Jose.
How to like broccoli, asparagus, cauliflower, Brussels
   sprouts.
How to perform a tea ceremony.

But you do have to know,
if you want your hair to stand on end,
and the truth Keats stumbled upon,
if not how to read a poem,
at least how to hear one.

A Dice Game

A dice game on a dark night,
that's the thing.

You shake, you rattle, you roll
and only barely can you see the numbers.

When it comes to Satori,
"I'm like a one-eyed cat, peepin' in a seafood
    store."

You Have Too Much

"You have too much investment in 'I.'
It's always 'I',
'I', 'I.' What about
yonder mountain? The tea leaves?
The caterpillar
your bicycle tire just ran over?
What about blue,
or blue and green,
and for that matter,
Washington's face on a dollar?

Who is this 'I'
you're always talking about?
Why don't you know?
Can't you do better?"

"I . . . I . . . I . . . ,"
the poor disciple stammered.

Of Mazu

Of Mazu, the Chan Patriarch, it is told,
"he had the piercing gaze of a tiger,
and walked ambling like a cow,"
which is a wonderful way of Zen walking.
Would you like to meet this fellow
who kicked and beat and insulted his
    disciples,
yelling into one poor unfortunate's ears,
    "Ho!"
so loudly the disciple was deaf for three
    days,
but then received insight?
Would you put Mazu on daytime national
    TV
or would you dismiss him
and send him to some crazy farm?
What is the price you'd pay to be
    enlightened,
and have you paid it yet?

How Can I Keep Them Together

How can I keep them together,
the child's wonder,
the adult's skills?

Risk within reason.
Open yourself within reason,
let reason open you.

Unlock the door from inside
with the same key that let you in.

Swing
on the door's hinges.

Annoyance

The secret of giving compliments
is not unlike metonymy
and synecdoche,
one part
standing for the whole
and thus it's not
"I loved your book"
but "I especially liked
the orange kittens in the applesauce."
Nor is it "good party"
but "the hot dog hor d'ouvres—
most exceptional!"

However, since
we're being discursive,
there's a definite risk
that praising one thing
might be misinterpreted
as damning another:
The gray shadows in the alley were awful.
The potato salad stank.
You must, therefore,
always remember
both forest and trees,

the ones in the other,
in the other, the ones,
finally, both together:
Great day!
The ants climbing up the log.

I Like Things

I like things out of the blue,
Alice blue,
Cambridge blue,
Carolina blue.

Cerulean, Cobalt blue,
Cornflower, Cyan, Denim,
Electric, Eton, Federal,
Han, and Iceberg blue.

Indigo, Klein,
Inkblue, Maya, Midnight blue,
Persian, Powder, Prussian,
Sapphire, Steel, Ultramarine,
Tiffany, and Blue Sky.

At the end of a koan, may I be smitten
by a lightning bolt out of blue sky.

Reminiscence

Once upon a time,
there was a Zen sign
at every small railroad crossing in America:

Stop. Look. And Listen.

On a side dirt road
outside Mechanicville, New York,
in my father's black Ford,
once we did that
for more than a half hour.

Boxcar after boxcar
appearing through the dark pines,
disappearing into the dark pines.

Achison, Topeka, and Santa Fe.
Delaware and Hudson.
Erie Lackawanna.
Rock Island Line.

We were listening to Johnny Cash
on our old car radio,
boxcars drifting by.

Here, I Shall Dwell

Here, I shall dwell in the rain.

Here, I shall watch the rain come down
   upon me,
through the branches of willows.

Here, I shall look out across Thrushwood
   Lake,
watching the wild geese appear and vanish.

Here, I shall dwell in the rain
as others have dwelt before me.

Here, I shall lift my hands to the rain
falling on my palms, running down my
   forearms.

Here, I shall dwell in the rain.
I shall dwell here in the rain.

You May Leave a Memory,
Or You Can Be Feted by Crows

Three years Huang Gongwang
worked on his famous handscroll,
Dwelling in the Fuchun Mountains.

As he put successive applications of ink to
    paper
over the "one burst of creation," his original
    design,
it is said he often sang like a tree frog
and danced on his old bare feet.

One day, he adds one hemp fiber stroke,
the next a moss dot.

What patience he had,
like a cat who comes back season after season
    to a mole's tunnel.

Honors may go to others.
Riches may go to others.
Huang Gongwang has one great job to do.

And he sings like a tree frog,
and he dances on old bare feet.

What Good Is Zen

What good is Zen
if it won't help my dying friend?

What good is Zen
if it can't stop an oil spill into the Gulf of
    Mexico?

What good is Zen
if I'm shot down in Afghanistan?

What good is Zen
if I'm broke and living on orange peels?

What good is Zen
in the windows of an abandoned house?

What good is Zen
if all it means is a pebble on the beach?

What good is Zen
if you imagine you've done nothing wrong?

Fortune Cookie Master

It amuses me, he said, to call them
"Cookies of Fortune." But then,
we turn everything around,
don't we? To understand it
(although you'll never understand it
for if you did, you'd not understand it),
practice making palindromes,
did, dad, toot, kayak, radar,
wet sanitary rat in a stew,
Do geese see God?
I'm alas, a salami,
or turning teacups upside down
so that Nothing spills out. Stop trying
to make sense of your life. Yes,
that would make sense, wouldn't it?
About as much sense as fortune cookies,
sweet crunchy American life.

The Constant Sound

What is it?
The constant sound of water running off
the mountain.
What is it?
A cricket making its way across the floor.

or

What is it?
The constant sound of water running off
the mountain.
What is it?
A cricket making its way across the floor.

Gaze

A single blind tortoise
swimming in a vast ocean
surfaces only once
every century.

Floating on the vast ocean
is a single golden yoke.

It is more rare,
said the Buddha,
to be reborn human
than for the tortoise
to surface with its head
poking through the hole
in the golden yoke.

You have this rare time.
Do not squander your chance
on the ephemeral.

Gaze
at the waves on the water.

One Day You Wish Yourself Dead

One day you wish yourself dead,
the next, alive.

Dead. Alive.
Alive. Dead.

One day you see yourself hanging
from a cottonwood tree, as in a western
    movie.
The next day you're riding a roller-coaster,
holding on with one hand, eating cotton
    candy with the other.

Dead. Alive.
Alive. Dead.

One day you're lying in a coffin,
no voices above you, but a mosquito
    trapped there also.
The next day you take your first picture
with a Kodak box camera.

Dead. Alive.
Alive. Dead.

One day you're heading west to a sixties band
    singing "Mother Earth."
The next day you're out of it forever,
floating among the stars, not one of which
    you can name.

A Basketball Game

Don't prefer one sense over another,
try to balance them,
creating a zone defense:
forwards, center, guards
shifting back and forth and up and down
    the court
against all distractions,
the crowd cheering
but you so alert
you hear nothing from the stands.

Concentrate. Absolute Nothing.

Keep your eyes on the ball.

Legend Has It

Legend has it that the monk Kukai
not only threw a thunderbolt from the shores
   of China
to land at Mt. Koya, in Japan,
where he set up a monastery,
but also a second *vajra*
which landed in a Kansas cornfield
to be discovered by Jack Kerouac and his
   friends
just hitchhiking along the road
on their way to San Francisco,
without a car in sight.

What a Long Conversation

What a long conversation
we never had!

All those rivers
we never crossed together.

You so busy with your own life,
I so busy with mine.

The Secret Is to Leap

The secret is to leap
widely and strangely
over the deep,
not knowing
what's down there,
but pretty certain
in some crevice
there must be a small
purple flower.

Unaccountable Days

It's true, they went like the wind,
but they also went like the blue sky some-
    times does
out over the Atlantic,
as well as cloud drifts, bamboo forests,
those many songs you barely notice.

It's true, they went like the wind
and are nowhere to be found in attic
    or cellar,
but they also sat down at quiet tables
and drank quiet coffee, and engaged
in the kind of quiet talk that calls for soft
    erasers.

It's true, they went like the wind,
but who would bring them back,
or who would lead them toward a secret
    passage,
those unaccountable days,
days only you have lost.

To Get Ahead

To get ahead,
do we really have to eat each other
as Balzac said,
"like spiders in a teapot"?

Suppose there is only
tea in the teapot,
being poured slowly
into many cups.

Listening Deeply

Listening deeply,
sometimes—in another—you can hear
the sound of a hermit, sighing
as he climbs a mountain trail to reach
    a waterfall
or a Buddhist nun reciting prayers
while moonlight falls through the window
    onto an old clay floor,
and once in a while, a child
rolling a hoop through the alleyways of
    Tokyo, laughing,
or a farmer pausing in a rice field to watch
    geese fly,
the thoughts on his lips he doesn't think
    to say.

As Han-Shan Observed

As Han-Shan observed,
sometimes there is no Zen
only hermits plodding up and down Cold
    Mountain,
the taste of lotus petals,
sometimes one of those rains
that make you think of stooped shoulders.

The Tribute

Throw pots,
Alan Watts.

Thanks, lots,
Alan Watts.

"Zen rocks,"
said Alan Watts.

Alan Watts
untied knots.

"Disconnect dots,"
said Alan Watts.

Everything rots,
including Alan Watts.

When Your Enthusiasm Dies

When your enthusiasm dies,
and it's just you staring at a stone
you kicked down some dark highway,

when you can't understand what you found
    in something:
that haiku by Basho,
The Brandenburg Concertos,
Turner's sea paintings,
even the smell of lilacs,
the taste of buckwheat pancakes with maple
    syrup,

just keep staring at the stone.

A Lesson

To test a flower arrangement,
photograph it in black and white.

A good arrangement will photograph
very effectively.

An arrangement strong in colors
but weak in design

will make a very poor
black and white photograph.

How may this lesson
elsewhere be applied?

A Tanka

The kind of green moss
patina on these old stone
New England fences
seems to deepen in autumn,
baked in the slow fading light.

It Isn't Going to Get Any Better

It isn't going to get any better,
    is it?

Then you might as well accept rock fences
and snakes living inside them.

It's going to get worse,
sometimes by inches, sometimes by days,
    isn't it?

Then you might as well take the elevator up to
    the top floor,
then take the elevator down.

It's going to get cold, and rainy or snowy,
    and dreary,
and you're going to feel like sobbing, aren't
    you?

Then you might as well throw your arms wide
    apart
and pray to anything above you, which is
    looming.

Minute to Minute

Minute to minute,
hour to hour,
day to day. . . .

Do you know how hard
it is to live
this Way?

Does the Spoon Perceive the Soup?

Does the spoon perceive the soup?
Does the rake perceive the leaves it rakes?
Does the sock perceive the foot as it enters?
Does the car perceive the man who drives
    the car?

Does the mountain feel the one who climbs
    the mountain?
Does the sea take umbrage from the fish
    within it?
Does the bed rejoice when lovers lie upon it?
Does the grave take notice when the body
    enters?

Is there a bell that hears its own ringing?
Will pockets shy from every coin they hold?
Can the laying on of hands make any
    difference?
Do words hear themselves?

Yes / No   No / Yes

As in a square dance,
twirl them around and do-si-do,
link hands and find your way home.

Not Why, But What

Not why, but *what,*
that's the secret
of Zen.

Not because,
but *is:*

the famous cherry blossom
blossoming.

Road Trip Song

Sorrow and pain, sorrow and pain.
Where there are clouds, there will be rain.

If there's no loss, there'll be no gain.
What you think is a road is only a lane.
You can't achieve wisdom
    from brewers' grain,
nor get yourself *noir*
    from cut sugar cane.
Don't take the side road,
    shoot down the Main.
Where have you placed
    your own weather vane?
It's greed and desire
    that brings sorrow and pain.

Sorrow and pain, sorrow and pain.
Where there are clouds, there will be rain.

Some Places for Prayer

A hovel.
A mountain shack.
A forest ranger's cabin.

A house made of plywood.
A house made of tin.
A cave.
A hut.
A tent in the wind.

A cabin.
A lean-to.
A shanty.
A shed.

A roof and four walls.
A refuge.
A place to lie down in.

The Taoist, Pausing

The Taoist, pausing
on the footpath that morning

suddenly aware with all his being
of the ten thousand things,

lichens, crystals, dewdrops, cobwebs,
pinpricks, paint dabs,

shading his eyes
against the sunrise,

told by every stone and branch and leaf
that the meeting place of Heaven and Earth

has always been the human body,
quietly

gives thanks to all the ten thousand
combinations,

mountains, oak trees, hummingbirds,
sparrow cries, ice cream flavors swirled

in such patterns and ripples and rhythms
all about him

I give thanks!
I give thanks!

on the footpath that morning,
the Taoist, pausing.

Chanced Upon

. . . these five pebbles
scattered below the surface
of the Farmington River,
I find, walking out.

. . . these three autumn leaves
fallen from a Japanese maple
upon the moss—
scarlet, mint-green, rust.

. . . the Buddha seated
among many flowers,
as a lawn ornament
at a house where children play.

. . . one hermit thrush,
singing, then stopping, then singing again
as you enter its forest,
and others reply.

Pondering Kuai-Shan

One day
you will lie in sickness
flat on your back,

thinking and pondering
from morning to night,
your heart full of dread.

The road ahead
vague, boundless.
Where will you go?

A pitcher of water
beside your bed,
a book you'll not finish.

In the dark room
digital clock
numbers floating.

"Nurse! Nurse!"
your mind will call,
"Nurse! Nurse!"

No one will come
into your room
. . . but the moon and the sun.

Songbirds Brush

Songbirds brush rooftops as they fly.

Crisscrossing the pond,
fish push aside stems of water-weeds.

Yesterday, tramping fields,
or swerving through city streets,
what did you scrape or bend
when you passed by?

Years and Years

Years and years and years. It takes
years and years and years
to get things simple:
an *enso*,
turning the tea cup three times,
bowing,
greetings, farewells.

Escape

On one of those days
when you don't wish to do anything
you have to do,

your resentment against duty, obligation,
expectation seething inside you,

sometimes you can't help yourself
and take revenge upon yourself
by doing nothing at all

except useless things
that count for nothing
and get you nowhere,

or you can hitch a ride
into the city
and lose yourself among its many lights.

Seeing

To take a photograph,
"Simplify. Simplify. Simplify,"
as Thoreau said.

A leaf or two upon a lazy river,

one raspberry,
or blueberry,
or strawberry
carelessly abandoned
on a white dinner plate,

a snowdrift, a boulder,

the hand of a Buddha statue touching earth—
nothing else, just the Buddha's hand,

this snapshot
of something just stumbled upon,

or this composition
meditated over for hours
until the light fits perfectly
into its shadows.

More Don't Know

When "Don't know"
swallows the entire universe
where will you be?

Going to Jackson?

Don't know. Don't know.

Eating fruit-on-the-bottom yogurt?

Don't know. Don't know.

"What you don't know won't harm you"—
is this true?

Don't know. Don't know.

Burning Duality

Burning duality
is a lot like burning trash.
You start with a lighter flame,
applying it to the edges,
then wait until it catches
before you step back
when it spreads to the core.

What does it leave?

Smoke.
Heat.
Ash.

What Did You Kill

What did you kill today?
A spider?
A fly?
A song halfway through itself?
A peanut butter and jelly sandwich?
Some mood that just happened to be
    walking in the rain?
The part of yourself that snaps fingers?

What did you kill it with?
A look?
Knives?
Laughter?
Bananafish?
The thought of a road that no one ever
    traveled?

Words Collected

Clay.
Straw.
Paper.
Wood.
Bamboo.
Stone.
Water.
Light.
Green.
Gray.
White.
Beige.
Sliding doors.
Diffused light.
Niche.
Bonsai.
Hanging scroll.

There Are Many Secrets

There are many secrets, but here's one
from Arthur Murray:
"One, two, change direction."
That's it. He's talking about steps.
One, two, change direction.
Use it for brushstrokes in a watercolor
or for writing a poem.
Make your whole life
constantly surprising.

Claim

Some claim
there can be no mastery in the art of the
   haiku
until the poet reaches sixty-five,

for only then will she or he have seen
enough cherry blossoms falling
and placed the rim of a tea cup against the lips
   enough times

to say that one breath
of a haiku in spring is
enough for one life.

Five Poems

Small Poem

The cardinal
in the snow.
Recall it
at will.

Small Poem Reversed

Recall it
at will:
The cardinal
in the snow.

Tiny Poem

Cardinal
In the snow.

Very Tiny Poem

Cardinal.
Snow.

Poem

Snow.

Rewriting a Poem
of Seasons by Seung Sahn

Purple violets in the spring grass.
In the summer, porch swings at night.
Vermont red and orange mountains.
The white-on-white of ski tracks
     in winter snow.

Is the world giving up on me?
Am I giving up on the world?
I sit bare-headed in the zazen room.
I find I don't care.

One jumbo jet in the blue sky.
Soda pouring from a McDonald's soda
     fountain.
The wind through the abandoned factories
     of Ansonia.
I give my whole life to them.

Raking in a Japanese Sand Garden

I'm not wearing a robe,
and my head's not shaven,
nor am I trying to solve
some impossible koan.

And it's been months
since I last meditated
or, in a small tea ceremony,
patiently waited.

Yet slowly, backing away
from one more life boulder,
I become calm, raking around it
a curving sand river

quietly flowing,
and the leaves falling here.

As I Cut Down the Forest of Desires

As I cut down the forest of desires,
clearing the underbrush,
partridge, grouse, and wild turkey
running before me,
I lift the back of my right arm to my forehead,
wiping the sweat away.

More and More

More and more, I've found myself
liking the places in between
stopping and starting
more than what I'm getting at:

the ten-minute drive to the store
more than shopping its aisles,

the walk to a neighbor's house
more than the neighbor,

putting off opening the newspaper
more than reading the news,

anticipating the nap,
more than stretching out upon the couch
and pulling over myself
a Hudson's Bay blanket,

not checking the email
until it's so piled up
it's bound to contain
really fine clusters,

after things are set in motion,
when it's too late to turn back,
those places without strings
where harm seldom comes.

A Prayer Box

What shall I put in the Gau?
Prayers? A Dzi bead from Taiwan?
A single grain of rice, such as the one
that fed Buddha each day?
A BB?
A leaf—and never open the box
to see if the leaf withered
(i.e., Schrödinger's Cat)?

What constitutes prayers these days?

Christians Say

Christians say,
"Could you completely calm your soul
you'd hear God whispering to you
well-nigh incessantly."

It would be like, I think,
becoming aware of all the waves—
    radio, TV, and cell phone—
constantly passing through our bodies,
how bathed we are in them,

that static, that blur

and then hearing,
as in a heavy rainfall,
the plash of a single stone
someone unaccountably cast
upon the still waters.

For Fifty Years Now

For fifty years now, I've been hounded
by Robert Creeley's lines,
"If you were going to get a pet,
what kind of animal would you get?"
So dumb, so corny, so zany
with those wriggling iambs and anapests,
and such simple rhymes.
I've been driven crazy,
crazy.

Maybe a cocker spaniel,
a Doberman pincher,
or golden retriever,
a wabi-sabi tabby,

a chipmunk not named "Alvin,"
a parrot that sings "Who are you?
I really want to know."
A horse descended from James Wright's
      pasture,
a koi, lots of koi, in a pond
in a Japanese garden,
swimming around and around
as if their happiness were mine.

Skin-Bag

What an ugly way to describe
this vessel that hold us.

Skin-bag.

Is this what I am?
Is this what you are?

Skin-bag.

I would rather have said,

Delusion that Bears My Name,
Beautiful Disguise,
Deceiver of Eyes,
Robe Draped Upon my Soul.

Turning Over the Tea Bowl

Turning over the tea bowl,
I found the nick
deliberately made—
the small flaw struggling against
beauty's arrogance.

When You Find the Tree

"When you find the tree with no shadow,
the ocean's waves all disappear,"
wrote Zen Master Kyong Ho,

who also wrote, "That's funny,
riding a cow, wanting to find a cow."

It's true, it's true:
Things having to do with each other
sometimes seem not to have anything
to do with each other,

like the cruel birds of North Dakota
and the fire escapes of the Bronx,

or that rock ledge out in the middle of
    Montana
called Pompey's Pillar,
cut into with the name of William Clark
we touched our fingers to one Autumn
as we had done
to the names on the Vietnam War Memorial,
including that of Captain Wayne Phillip
    Bundy

who taught me how to hold a cigarette
    properly
and smoke as if I knew what I was doing
in a college dormitory laundry room
so long ago you don't ever want to know,

his airplane down,
that life of his over.

In a World without Forests

In a world without forests,
where shall I find a forest?

In a world without forest streams from which
    to drink,
where shall I find forest streams from which
    to drink?

In a world without birds making calligraphy
    in the sky,
where shall I find calligraphy in the sky?

In a world where there is no silence,
where shall I find silence?

In a world where the chopping of the axe is
    not heard,
where shall I hear the chopping of the axe?

In a world where there is cry of neither wolf
    nor loon,
where shall I hear the cry of wolf or loon?

In a world where wildflowers do not grow
    for miles,
where shall I find wildflowers?

I Face the Image of the Buddha

I face the image of the Buddha
to deliver my sermon.

The Buddha's eyes are closed.
He's resting or sleeping.

Or meditating,
or thinking about what's on TV,
or of how many times hands open and
    close throughout the day,
or blue smoke upon the mountains.

He's not thinking about me.
I'm on my own.

Nonetheless, to deliver my sermon,
I face the image of the Buddha.

This Carnelian Mala

This carnelian mala,
as I round it this morning,
saying with each bead,
each surface that falls onto itself,
om mani padme hum, om mani padme hum,
how strange it first felt
twining itself, now and then,
around my wristwatch.

His Book

"I can only hear the locust
  chirring through the forest,"
Master Kakuan wrote,
unable to find the Self,
searching the wrong paths
for the wrong reasons.
*I can only hear the locust
chirring through the forest.*

If You Can Find the Door

If you can find the door to just one thing,
you will know all.

The door to the sports arena.
The door backstage.
The bedroom door.

Shall I open the door,
or shall I close it?

First you must find the door,
which may be suspended in the air above
    a high mesa,
or hidden in a city, beside the government.

If the door has a window,
should I look through it?

The door to the parking garage.
The door with a bar across it.
The door you push open with your shoulder.
The door that sticks.
The door that gives you away.

After Han-Shan, Again

Not one of the men who carried muskets
across the fields of Gettysburg
still kneels in the dusk.

Not one of the women who twirled parasols
and ripped up petticoats for bandages
still sobs on the veranda.

Morning after morning, violet petals fade
    and fall.
And here where I park my car was once
    a teeming forest.

Moment

Simply twist open the top of a jelly jar,
mindful of the pads of your thumb and fingers
applying pressure, and at the same time
the stubbornness of your other hand gripping
what's most likely a cylinder,
holding the jar steady while your wrist turns
    right
until the **POP** as the vacuum seal is broken,
releasing the grape or cherry or orange
    marmalade
or peach or strawberry scent into the
    kitchen air.

Trying to Observe Again

This winter
the snow was the most ivory
I've ever seen it,

lying on the stone walls of New England—

something, I think,
about the color of the sky this winter,
the light so strangely faded, the cold
   continual,

                              an ivory

spread for miles across the roads and fields
you could almost bite into
like the inside of a toasted marshmallow

you might be happy to crawl deep deep
   down inside.

Words of Reassurance

You do not have a set time.
You may sit on a stone wall somewhere in
    New Hampshire.
You may drive the Interstate, holding a cup
    of Starbuck's.
You may drink a date milkshake in New
    Mexico.
You may lie in a closed velvet-lined coffin,
hearing voices above you.

You will change worlds in an instant.
Guishan Lingyou says, "We are like spring
    frost.
We are like morning dew."

The Flower Arranger's Instructions

Through elimination or placement,
create space.

Subtle simplicity,
where and what to cut. . . .

Is the space to be created
necessary or not?

Study each branch,
each flower.

      For instance

take the camellia branch in its natural state,
a mass of flowers and leaves.

Remove the unnecessary
flowers, leaves, and small branches.

By careful bending,
endow the branch with a pure line.

You now hold
an object of exquisite loveliness.

You have earned your right to say
exquisite loveliness.

Shaping

For the best bonsai,
roots must be exposed,
and crooked
like chicken feet.

It's all the better
if branches writhe.

The more you admit suffering,
the more you'll be alive.

Question Everything

Question everything,
even the question mark,
that shepherd's crook
floating in the air above
that small round rock.

If you—stubbornly—still
wish to be unhappy,
maybe you can grasp it.

Better yet,
chop a miracle
into egg salad,
which is what we have
in our knapsacks,
along with a pint apiece
of whole chocolate milk,
cream cheese, potato chips,
and a great deal of apple butter.

Covered by the Husk

Covered by the husk, the unhusked grain
seems not the rice.

Placed in a ceramic pot, a lamp
seems not to be lighted.

Mixed with milk, the essence of the butter
is scarcely tasted.

The net of afflictions, the net of afflictions,
how it falls upon us
who are all Buddhas, in essence.

The Grip

In the grip of sickness,
I lose all ambition,
the world is
fingers around my throat,
a thumb on my windpipe
and all I can think of is
how might I pry
that hand away.

If It's Not One Thing

If it's not one thing, it's another.
One thing, then another. They're not
going away.
You may heal, but more likely
you'll half-heal, or quarter-heal.
And as you get older,
two things, three things, everything
comes at you. . . . So it's no wonder,
if it brings you at least a little comfort,
you'll eat a jelly doughnut,
a cup of custard,
a peach.

Like my father, dying in the hospice,
with his pathetic M&M bribes to his
    nurses,
in lieu of what he couldn't do,
be amazed you've lasted
still one more day.

How Strange

How strange, how strange,
how strange it is,
this living, this dying,
along with buttercups,
bottlecaps,
the *pop, pop, pop* of colors in a supermarket
    aisle.

Gifts

I made this mala for you
while playing over and over,
my favorite songs,
each bead a mantra
absorbing the songs.

. . . a swiftly running mountain river
entering into a vast placid lake.

Songs from my childhood.
Songs from my teens.
Songs from my adulthood.
Songs from old age.

May you count them as yours.

As Long as I Wake Up

"As long as I wake up on this side of the grass,
I'm okay," I overheard someone tell someone
    else
in a supermarket aisle, but not wanting
to appear startled, I didn't turn around
until too late. Whoever he had been was gone
along with whoever had asked the usual
nearly automatic "How are you?" Beside me
tiered cans of Libby's vegetables and fruits
gleamed in their usual way along the shelves
of Stop and Shop. Outside the store windows,
it had begun to rain. A very few calm souls
walked slowly to the parking lot. Most others
    dashed,
pushing their shopping carts before them,
intent on getting home before the storm got
    worse.

Cat

"There's more to life than just
eat and sleep and play,"
        I tell my cat, who just
sits around all day,

        looks evil into the mirror,
swats butterflies in sleep,
        turns tail on the bathroom mirror,
thinks mice are his to keep,

        or torture, or nibble, or bat.
"There's more to life than food,
        curl up, stretch out, or bat
a mouse to Hell. You should

        know better, Cat, than that."
But as is "The Way of Cat,"
        which is to contemplate
and be in all ways *Cat,*

        no more, no less, he just
yawns and seems content
        with being only just
whatever *Is*—no bent

thing, he. . . then seems to say,
grow fat, sleep long, and when
you tire of that, I'd say,
"Well, then

it's time to play." And in
a nutshell, this is Zen.
Eat. Sleep. Play. Wise in
all things is my cat Zen.

Awakening the Fire

"Awakening the fire," I call it.
You listen to people, you listen so deeply
you can hear their past lives,
the crackle of their funeral pyres,
and see smoke rising over the Ganges,
and there it is, that individual spark
that makes one life unlike any other.
You tease it out. You blow on it. You fan it.
You offer it a handful of dried tinder.
But that's all you can do
and almost always
the spark glows momentarily and then
    returns to ash.
Not this life. Not this life. Not this life.
Not even the next.

Not Too Far from the Golden Gate

Just as a tree understands a tree's job,
and water understands water's job,
you will go to hell like an arrow
if you don't understand your job
is not to explain your situation and condition,
but, like a melon, to just grow and ripen
by yourself. The ocean is full of water.
There are many clouds in the sky.
What is the one pure and clear thing?

Lying Prone

You can wet your right index finger with
    your tongue.
You can wiggle your toes.
You can roll up your sleeves.
You can stroke your chin for no reason.

You can count the hairs on your arm and
    lose count.
You can bat your eyes many times in
    succession.
You can make and unmake a fist.
You can chase a sentence far out across a
    piece of paper.

You can run your tongue across your teeth.
You can touch your ears lightly for their
    pleasure.
You can wonder why no one gives their
    elbows names.
You can revel, once more, in your breathing.

Thirty Thousand Days

In the thirty thousand or so days,
more or less,
you have upon the planet Earth
if you're lucky,
how many did you spend
looking at pine trees
or sparrows blown by the eastern wind,
or labels on soup cans,
or the ways clothes hang on mannequins,
things like that?

Should You Come Across

Should you come across a stone Buddha in
    the field,
if it's covered with weeds,
clean the weeds off.

It's more than likely
you'll never come across a stone Buddha in
    the field.
All the more reason
to clean the weeds off.

A Harmony

Clouds are in the northern sky.
Rain is in the eastern sky.
The auto mechanic is working under the car.
The children return home from school.

Sickness Is My Companion

Sickness is my companion
that walks with me beside the sand garden
and follows me into the zendo room.

Death is my friend
that never leaves me to myself on a hilltop
and always awaits my footsteps.

The three of us,
sitting around a small table, sipping tea,
whispering among the rising fumes.

Exile

Should I give up on the world, asked the poet,
flee to the shelter of mountains, riversides, and
    farms,
drive aimlessly to a dead end in the road
and weep there?

Under the eastern hedge,
should I pick chrysanthemums?

At my late age,
should I attempt poems?

Yes.

Again, *Yes.*

How much is inevitable,
in how much there is no choice.

Water beside the Road

Not some river, just those lines of water
that follow a heavy rainstorm
carrying twigs the size of broken
    matchsticks,
a newly torn aspen leaf, a dandelion stem,
and dislodge here and there a pebble,
that's all. So small, they neither ripple
nor swell—just temporary lines beside a road,
lines you might or might not notice
    disappear
as you walk along, glad this rainstorm's over.

The World Delights

The world delights in vanity,
but here I am at Thrushwood Lake,
a lake so obscure that most maps don't show it.
Here I am turning my mala beads,
small flocks of wild geese
taking off or landing on the waters before me.
How slightly they disturb the waters.
What little difference they make.
You in Japan, in Russia, in China,
you don't know me, do you?
Only by accident have you come upon my
    words.

Eggshells Are So Light

Holding the shells of two eggs
in the palm of one hand,
I never in my life before
became aware
eggshells are so light.
Why, they're almost
as light as a Crayola mark.
Even when I move my head,
if I wasn't looking,
I doubt I'd know they were there,
and if this is so, what else
might I have missed,
like the teakettle whistle
at the end of the sound of "Yes,"
low-lying hills in the distance,
how the sky fits into them
like one hand pressing
into another,
the smell of a cloth bag filled
with quarters and dimes,
and at my age, how silly,
how splendid,
to still be discovering this.

Wild Geese

Wild geese
coming down from gray sky,
suddenly landing
at Thrushwood Lake
as if out of nowhere.

Suddenly I realize,
or is it remember,
everything, actually,
comes out of nowhere:

the North wind,
a hole in a stump,
two coals for a snowman's eyes,
a spoonful of sugar,
the pills I take,
everything I love and hate,
a scent
of caramel syrup . . .

wild geese

wandering, or a heart at rest?

How good
to have forgotten my camera.

I Would Like to Leave

I would like to leave my poems on mountain
    cliffs,
but there are no mountains here.

I would like to write my poems on rocks,
but the town would soon clean them,
    thinking them graffiti.

I want to put my poems on the sides of mud
    huts,
but there are no mud huts at Thrushwood
    Lake.

And my handwriting has no beauty to it.

Ten Years, Fifteen Years

Ten years, fifteen years,
hours from now, minutes from now,
I'll leave this world.

The body that contained me will fall,
but the wind will blow across Thrushwood
   Lake,
some child will be laughing.

It's the old familiar plaint, isn't it?
You live a little, you die, the world goes on.
It's the old familiar observation.

Did you write a sonnet?
Did you stand on your head and wriggle your
   toes?
Did you eat apricots?
Did you hold in your hand
red leaves and green moss?

Wild rose. Wild rose.

Today, I Looked

Today, I looked at a book of watercolor
    paintings.
Today, I petted a small gray-furred cat for
    ten minutes.
Today, I heard the red teakettle whistle.
Today, I napped and dreamed of golden
    umbrellas.
Today, I smelled incense burning by a
    Buddha statue.
Today, I tasted a rice cake and a drop of
    honey.

While you were rearranging the world,
while you were throwing people from
    sandstone cliffs,
while you were setting people up to ride
    in dirigibles,
while you were striding over the world
    in your seven-league boots,
while you were drinking huge gulps of the
    world's most wonderful dark red wine,
while you were writing yourself in history
    books and on granite monuments,

today, I strung the twenty-seven beads of a
    wrist mala,
today, I watched the amazing wind in an
    amazing Japanese maple,
today, I drew a small circle in the water of
    Thrushwood Lake,
today, I saw a cardinal perched on a garage
    rooftop,
today, I spent an hour staring into Nothing,
today, I felt a couch with my whole body.

Releasing Life

Because you must seek food constantly,
because you must constantly avoid being
    food,
because you cannot speak,
because you cannot understand language
and therefore cannot take refuge in the
    three jewels
although you, too, live in the presence
    of the dharma,

Bird, I preach to you,
I free you.

Turtle, I preach to you,
I free you.

Fish, I preach to you,
I free you

here, on Thrushwood Lake's edges,
under the pines and the willows.

How Long Shall I Wait

How long shall I wait
beside this small lake

envying the high clouds?

The passage my life opened
is closing soon.

How have I walked it?

I remember brushing both hands
against stone walls

and the Buddha's last words.

so often translated,
translated in so many ways.

Acknowledgments

My great thanks to the editors of the following, who first published some of these poems: *The American Poetry Review, The Buddhist Poetry Review, The Hudson Review, The New Criterion, On Barcelona, Poetry, Rattle, Tricycle.*

And to my wife, L. N. Allen, and to Cortney Davis—my two first readers.

And to Wisdom's Editorial Director Josh Bartok and to Wisdom's Maura Gaughan, for their encouragement, patience, and exceptional advice and suggestions that helped shape this manuscript. *Zen Master Poems* is their book, also.

About the Author

Dick Allen (b. 1939) is variously known as a mystical poet, a Zen Buddhist poet, a poet concerned with the turn of the twenty-first century, a poet of contemporary science, and a poet whose style ranges from formal to free verse. Having published eight volumes of poetry and numerous poems in publications such as *The New Yorker*, *The Atlantic Monthly*, *The Hudson Review*, and *The American Poetry Review*, Allen has served as Connecticut's State Poet Laureate for five years and has won prizes and praise for his poetry nationwide. With his wife Lori, also a writer, Dick Allen lives, writes, and takes walks besides Thrushwood Lake in Trumbull, Connecticut.

Also Available
from Wisdom Publications

The Wisdom Anthology of North American Buddhist Poetry
Andrew Schelling

"Nothing else comes close."—*Pacific Rim Review of Books*

Awesome Nightfall
The Life, Times, and Poetry of Saigyō
William Lafleur

"Saigyō's poems are masterful mind-language challenges. Bill LaFleur's deeply understanding translations present us with the snake-like energy of the syntax, and the illuminated world that was called out by one man's lifetime of walking and meditation is again right here."
—Gary Snyder, poet and activist

Everything Yearned For
Manhae's Poems of Love and Longing
Francisca Cho

Winner of the Daesan Foundation Literary Award

When I Find You Again, It Will Be in Mountains
The Selected Poems of Chia Tao
Mike O'Connor

"A gorgeous tapestry."—Anne Waldman, Naropa University

Where the World Does Not Follow
Buddhist China in Picture and Poem
Translated and Introduced by Mike O'Connor
Photography by Steven Johnson

"The poetry and photographs, equally captivating, take the reader on a guided tour of China."—*Foreword*

The Clouds Should Know Me by Now
Buddhist Poet Monks of China
Edited by Mike O'Connor and Red Pine
Introduced by Andrew Schelling

"Here is a breathtaking millennium of Buddhist poet-monks."—*Inquiring Mind*

Daughters of Emptiness
Poems of Chinese Buddhist Nuns
Beata Grant

"This beautiful book testifies to the power of
Buddhist practice to nourish the human spirit
even when war, physical hardship, class discrimi-
nation, and oppression seem insurmountable."
—Grace Schireson, author of *Zen Women*

About Wisdom Publications

Wisdom Publications is the leading publisher of classic and contemporary Buddhist books and practical works on mindfulness. To learn more about us or to explore our other books, please visit our website at wisdompubs.org or contact us at the address below.

Wisdom Publications
199 Elm Street
Somerville, MA 02144 USA

We are a 501(c)(3) organization, and donations in support of our mission are tax deductible.

Wisdom Publications is affiliated with the Foundation for the Preservation of the Mahayana Tradition (FPMT).